The Torchbearers

The Olympic Torch
in
Peterborough

By Brian Holdich

By the same Author

My Indian Journey
India Revisited
The 2001 New York City Marathon
Stanground Boy
The Man from the Pru

Published in Great Britain
By Brian's Books (B.W. Holdich)
Market Deeping
Peterborough
Cambridgeshire
PE6 8JN

ISBN 978 0 9521017 5 8
The Torchbearers

Printed and bound by Spiegl Press Ltd
Guash Way, Stamford, Lincs PE9 1XH

COMMENTS

The Olympic Torch's arrival in the City, 3rd July 2012 taken from *The Peterborough Telegraph* :

This was a once in a life-time event for the city and was enjoyed by thousands of residents and will last long in their memory, and we have been overwhelmed with the volume of people who have supported this event, this was without doubt record numbers for Peterborough and even the national organisers didn't anticipate these numbers. Peterborough's done us proud.

Head of Commercial Operations at Peterborough City Council – Annette Joyce

This has been one of the best days in the city's history that we have ever had with crowds of people turning out to support the Torchbearers and the Olympics. It was stunning to walk around and see people's faces and I've been really taken aback by the amount of people seen. I also want to thank my team who have done a brilliant job as it's been a remarkable team effort.

Peterborough City Council Chief Executive – Gillian Beasley

The atmosphere within the crowds was just incredible as everyone wanted to see the Torchbearers carrying the Olympic Torch with such pride on behalf of Peterborough, and the entertainment laid on for the children in Cathedral Square and the Embankment made the day so very special.

Peterborough Councillor – Janet Goodwin

FOREWORD

My first contact with Brian Holdich was way back in the late 1950's to early 1960's when we played football together for Glinton in the Peterborough league when over the following years our paths would occasionally cross. Then in the year 2012-2013 I was elected Mayor of Peterborough when during my term of office one of the most pleasant of official duties was to travel part of the way on the Nene Valley Railway between Wansford and Peterborough with the Olympic flame in a lantern on a railway carriage table directly where my wife and myself were sitting. The outcome of seeing the Olympic flame was wonderful as the flame had already visited many areas on its journey across the UK in preparation for when the Olympic Torch would light the cauldron at the opening ceremony of the London 2012 Olympic Games.

Brian being a Torchbearer was also involved in the same event where along with others he was to carry the Olympic Torch on its journey to Peterborough, where our paths were to cross again, and where we would both share many exciting memories of a very special day with enormous crowds watching the proceedings. Because of such a memorable day Brian has been obliged to go into print once more to savour the many incredible moments before all is forgotten. I thoroughly enjoyed reading this book about the Torchbearers as I'm equally sure others will too. I wish Brian every possible success with the publication of this book.

George Simons
Past Mayor of Peterborough City May 2012 - May 2013

I dedicate this book to the 8,000 Torchbearer's where their very presence of carrying the Olympic Torch across the UK was a spectacular success, being the ideal preparation for the forthcoming London 2012 Olympic Games.

The Author

Tash Applegate with Lord Coe

Four cricketers wives of Market Deeping Cricket Club prepare to give Brian Holdich a rousing send-off in St. John's Street, Peterborough. Left to right. Barbara Buckley, Lesley Evans, Mary Burton and Sandra Jones.

CONTENTS

ACKNOWLEDGEMENTS

First on my list of thanks must be the International Olympic Committee for giving me permission to quote from certain pages of the London 2012 Olympic Torch Relay Handbook.

I am much indebted to the past Mayor of Peterborough, George Simons who kindly agreed to write the Foreword to the book. Grateful thanks must go to Sandra Jones who nominated me to be a Torchbearer and also to thank David Seymour of the Peterborough Telegraph for his help. I do indeed thank Anita Randall who was involved with the typing and layout of the manuscript. Not forgotten is Annette Joyce, Head of Commercial Operations at Peterborough City Council and Gillian Beasley, City Council Chief Executive who along with Councillor Janet Goodwin allowed me to put into print their comments, which were given to the Telegraph on seeing the Olympic Flame on its arrival in Peterborough on 3rd July 2012. Special mention and sincere praise must go to eight Torchbearers being John Peake, Nick Haste, Mike Russell, Alice Evans, Sumayya Manji, Steve Berridge, Iain Crighton and Tash Applegate being part of the same Torch Relay Team as myself who were able to write their own particular story of such an historic day, which I believe has captured the essence, considerably more so with their own experiences.

Finally my appreciation for publishing this book goes to Spiegl Press of Stamford.

INTRODUCTION

Being picked as a Torchbearer for the London 2012 Olympic Games on 3rd July 2012 has left me with many treasured memories of a fabulous day, and even now, many months later, I can still visualise the scene as I have to pinch myself that I really did participate in such an event. I carried the Olympic Torch in front of record amounts of people in Peterborough who had come to see the Olympic Torch and I regard this as a very great honour indeed. Looking back on my life as a young boy growing up in Stanground, Peterborough I was sports mad (much to the detriment of my school work) and not for one single moment would I ever think that years later I would be carrying the Olympic Torch for the forthcoming Olympic Games. Playing cricket and football in the green fields of Stanground it was instilled in me at a very early age at school that whatever sport I chose to play I was to play within the correct spirit of the game, which meant in a sportsman like manner with the attitude of fair play and correctness. Although I always wanted to win, defeat was accepted gracefully, and surely this is what those high principles of the Olympic Games are all about which very much represents those Olympic values of respect, excellence and friendship.

I decided to write this book (albeit only a short story) about six months after being a Torchbearer, but it's been a real struggle and I have to admit it has caused many headaches being hesitant at times whether I should continue or not. The reason for this being that how could I possibly write about a subject that only lasted twelve minutes? This was the amount of time I would be carrying the Olympic Torch and I've regarded the writing of such a book as a real challenge. The main reason however for writing this book is that to my knowledge no full length account has ever been written by any such author who has been a Torchbearer for the Olympic Games. Obviously many an article would have been written but never a full-blown narrative in the form of a book where just maybe I could be the first.

I hope this book gives a clear indication and captures the imagination of the reader into what it meant to be a Torchbearer carrying, with pride, the Olympic Torch on what was a most extraordinary day. A day where tumultuous crowds created an incredible atmosphere which, to put it mildly, was simply sensational, where the clapping and applause never seemed to stop, with red, white and blue union jacks being waved everywhere along the route which made one proud to be British and very patriotic too. Being a Torchbearer in the Olympic Torch relay team would play an important role in getting the UK ready to celebrate the opening of the games, when the Olympic flame would come to the end of its long 70 day journey, when the very last Torchbearer would light the cauldron at the opening ceremony in the new Olympic stadium in London on 27th July 2012.

It was nearer to the publication date of this book that I had a change of heart by altering the title from The Torchbearer to The Torchbearers, strictly for the reason that ten other Torchbearers in our group on that memorable day have become part of my story, even more so when I was able to get the majority of their comments in print. I've really appreciated their observations which are remarkably like my own, but seen through different eyes. As I'm sure the other 8,000 Torchbearers all over Great Britain have their own particular tale to tell, this therefore is one such Torchbearers own story.

A Momentous Occasion

I've been involved with many different charities over the years and have managed to raise certain amounts of money where I have persuaded people to sponsor me on my marathon walks. I must admit though to being very surprised when I was nominated to carry the Olympic Torch in Peterborough on 3rd July 2012, when the Olympic flame would be arriving in the city on its journey over vast areas of the UK. I did have certain reservations and even misgivings that surely there were far more deserving people than myself to carry the Olympic Torch in what was going to be undoubtedly a momentous occasion, one where Great Britain would play host in the most important role in getting ready to celebrate the opening of the Olympic Games on 27th July. My name had been put forward for being a Torchbearer along with 8,000 others from the UK, who would have all been nominated, like myself, to carry the Olympic Torch. And so it was that on 20th March 2012 I received notification in the form of an official letter from the Olympic Torch Relay Committee confirming that I'd been selected to be a Torchbearer. I really was quite exhilarated on hearing such news as this was what I'd been waiting for and I was already beginning to look forward to when I'd be carrying the Olympic Torch. I was as pleased as punch as anyone could possibly be.

Market Deeping in Lincolnshire, being eight miles from Peterborough, is where I've lived with my family for 36 very enjoyable years. So when I was informed I was going to be a Torchbearer I quite naturally assumed that this small market town would be where I'd be carrying the Olympic Torch, particularly as the torch relay route would virtually pass through the centre of the town. However, I was really disappointed to learn I'd be carrying the torch in Peterborough not Market Deeping. I really did my utmost to try to get it moved but the Olympic authorities wouldn't budge by stating that as I was born in Peterborough it had been decided that that's where I should be. So I had to settle for my walk to be in Peterborough, but rather than dwell too much on that decision it quickly became apparent that it was definitely better to carry the Olympic Torch anywhere than not at all, and I do know however I was still chuffed to bits – after all Peterborough was my birthplace and I've always been proud to have been born there. Any disappointment I originally had meant that it was subsequently dismissed straight away.

The Olympic Flame

The 2012 Olympic flame had arrived in the UK on 18th May 2012 after being lit by the sun's rays in a temple in Hera, Olympic Greece, and it was in a traditional ceremony in the ruins of the home of the ancient games that on 19th May the Olympic flame started on its 70 day journey across Great Britain. Passing triumphantly through large and deliriously happy crowds the Olympic flame visited 1,000 cities, towns and villages coming to within an hour of 95% of the population on its journey. It really did seem as though virtually everyone wanted to see the Olympic Torch in the UK. The Olympic flame would eventually end when the last Torchbearer would light the cauldron at the opening ceremony, where the torch relay team would play a prominent role in helping to get the UK ready to celebrate the Olympic Games.

The triangular shape of the Olympic Torch, which I was to carry was inspired by a series of threes and are to be found in the history of the games with the Vision of the Olympic movement, these being the values of Respect, Excellence and Friendship. These three words make up the Olympic motto of Faster, Higher and Stronger. The Vision of the London 2012 Olympic Games was to combine the three bodies of work being Sport, Education and Culture. This also meant it was the third time that London had hosted the Olympic Games, those times being 1908, 1948 and now 2012. The Olympic Torch was designed by a London design company with the 8,000 cut out circles on the torch which represented each of the actual 8,000 Torchbearers who would carry the flame across many areas of the UK. With the circles running the whole length of the torch enabling each Torchbearer to see the burner system that would keep the flame alight, also ensuring the torch didn't get too hot.

Made of brass and coloured gold to embrace the qualities of the Olympic flame, the Olympic Torch was a magnificent looking structure which cost over £400 to make, being 800mm high and weighing nearly 1kg with the burner system installed.

A Very Special Day

So the great day being 3rd July had finally arrived and after a good night's sleep, eating a hearty breakfast and reading the daily newspaper I knew in my bones that this day was going to be a very special day. I couldn't concentrate on anything in view of what was in front of me and as the morning progressed slowly I was becoming extremely restless, getting more fidgety by the second as I just wanted to get the morning over as quickly as possible, knowing that later that afternoon, in all probability, was going to be one of greatest of days imaginable that I was ever likely to encounter. I couldn't seem to control my emotions – being excited one minute and uncertain the next. I was even asking myself what would happen if on my walk I dropped the torch and the flame went out, which I am sure would make me look the biggest fool imaginable.

Nerves I know can strike at any time, regardless of whatever one's age is likely to be and often I would be lacking in self-confidence. Where I had experienced similar feelings with every sport I ever played going back to when I was a youngster, and sometimes just thinking about what is required to do did not fill me with confidence, so this particular day would prove to be no exception, which meant that this day was certainly not going to be any different from those other nerve wracking days. But surely, I said to myself, I had to get a firm grip of the proceedings and try to enjoy such a wonderful occasion and if at all possible remain cool, calm and collected.

Briefed in the Key Theatre

The allocation collection point where I had to report to was the Key Theatre at the river embankment in Peterborough where I had to present myself for 3.00pm wearing my white coloured uniform which had previously been sent to me by the sports company Samsung who were the main sponsors of the Olympic Torch relay team. I don't mind admitting that I felt rather proud to be wearing the symbols of the five Olympic rings on the front of my uniform. Samsung had insisted that no other clothes were to be worn over the uniform which considering they were the main sponsor was perfectly understandable. Once in the Key Theatre I had to prove my identity by producing my driver's licence because they would have no idea who I was, and it was in this theatre I was to meet the ten other Torchbearers who were part of the same relay team as myself. For some unknown reason one of the Torchbearers didn't turn up which would obviously create problems being one short, but with eleven of us all together we all seemed friendly and we got along reasonably well with conversation flowing comparatively easily. There was a vast difference in the ages of the eleven, the eldest being 87 years of age who was an Olympian himself, being a member of the great British hockey team which won a silver medal at Wembley in the 1948 Olympic Games. The youngest of our team relay group being a young schoolgirl of 14 years of age.

It was in the Key Theatre we had our very first look at the Olympic Torch which really was most impressive and would take pride of place in my home in Market Deeping. While still in the Key Theatre we were being briefed by a representative from Samsung who gave instructions on how to hold the torch correctly, irrespective of whether one walks or runs with their torch but to hold the torch high and well away from one's face. We were then informed of the procedure of how the torch relay team actually works and most importantly what happens at each of the exchange points when the changeover takes place. This is when the Olympic flame is passed from one Torchbearer to another Torchbearer which is so important to get it absolutely right. Most of all, the representative from Samsung told us to enjoy ourselves while carrying the Olympic Torch, "keep smiling and continue to wave to the crowds who will respond in the appropriate manner with much clapping and cheering".

The First Exchange Point

At 5.15pm the eleven Torchbearers departed from the Key Theatre and boarded a shuttle bus that had been parked outside the front of the theatre, where we were transported to our very first exchange point which was situated in Oundle Road. All shuttle buses all over the country were to play an important role in these Olympic Torch relays by dropping off each Torchbearer at their known exchange points. I'm sure as we boarded this shuttle bus all eleven of us must have wondered what was in store for us as our shuttle bus crossed over the city's river Nene and the railway bridges and then into Oundle Road, Woodston. Straight away it was most noticeable whilst on the bus that small groups of people were already gathering on the pavements of the road and having recognised us in our white uniforms began waving furiously to get our attention. The further our shuttle bus travelled along Oundle Road the larger the crowds seemed to be, it was as though our torch relay group had already started.

There were three exchange points on Oundle Road, which we would be using on returning to the city centre, the first one being at Orton Mere Railway Station situated near the Gordon Arms Public House. It was in the pub car park that our bus driver conveniently parked his shuttle bus and we sat patiently waiting for the Olympic flame to arrive on its journey from Wansford near the A1, where many Torchbearers would have been carrying the Olympic flame in their own torches. As the first Torchbearer to leave our shuttle bus would be number 89, this meant that 88 other Torchbearers had already that day carried the Olympic Torch. All the remaining Torchbearers on our shuttle bus would have their own numbers pinned to the front of their uniforms and our very last Torchbearer in our group would be number 100. This being the total amount of Torchbearers used every day throughout the UK. As we waited for the incoming Torchbearer to arrive please believe me when I say the excitement was just beginning.

Arrival of the Olympic Torch

The incoming shuttle bus would have travelled that morning from Leicester, passing through the town of Stamford and the historic grounds of Burghley House where the Olympic Torch would have been carried by many Torchbearers who were greeted by large and enthusiastic crowds. It was while we were parked in the Gordon Arms car park, still waiting for the previous Torchbearer to make his appearance, that, in next to no time at all, our shuttle bus was surrounded by literally hundreds of people with inquisitive eyes who seemed full of curiosity by staring at the Torchbearers on board. It was then that I realised how massively big this 2012 Olympic Torch relay was going to be and was sure to bring huge crowds, just like it had done all over the UK and where Peterborough wasn't going to be any different. It was then I thought of the younger girls on board our shuttle bus as they were beginning to show signs of nervousness, which was only to be expected in view of their age. Looking out from the shuttle bus windows to see such masses of people who had congregated at and around the Gordon Arms car park was astonishing to say the least.

It was then that our host from Samsung, who had travelled with us, began to brief us once again as regards to holding the Olympic Torch correctly, especially when the changeover occurs when the Olympic flame is transferred between two Torchbearers. Our host by this time could see that some of us on board were beginning to get slightly restless and I'm sure that all of us just wanted the whole show to get moving. I know I did as I couldn't wait to get my legs going as all the sitting on the shuttle bus and previously in the Key Theatre wasn't helping me at all. Not that I'd be running as those days had disappeared years ago but now being a walker my legs tend to stiffen up if I sit down for too long. Our host, in order for us to stay alert, wanted to know how we had been picked to be a Torchbearer and hopefully we gave him adequate answers. Finally he said "Remember to enjoy yourselves as this will be a day you will never forget". Someone on our bus then remarked "they are coming" which meant only one thing – the incoming Torchbearer was fast approaching with a great convoy of traffic following him.

The Kiss of Two Torches

Within minutes of hearing such news, our shuttle bus driver, with the help of the police, began to manoeuvre his bus from the pub car park. This was hardly an easy task with the massive crowds still gathered around, but manage it he did, and parked the bus near to our first exchange point on Oundle Road. By this time our first Torchbearer had been told to disembark from the bus carrying his Olympic Torch. Once off the bus an official guided him to where he would be situated on the side of the road where he waited for the incoming Torchbearer and the Olympic flame was transferred. Another official was on hand to see that the changeover was completed as smoothly as possible. The transfer of the flame was concluded with the tops of both torches being held briefly together where the cartridges on each torch automatically springs into action as the receiving cartridge is switched on to receive the flame, while the cartridge giving the flame is switched off. This intriguing exchange known as "The Kiss" was witnessed by hundreds of spectators. The exchange of the flame was really a simple process if done properly but done incorrectly the cartridges will not work – this being just one of the reasons for an official being present.

I've already mentioned that we as a group of Torchbearers were one Torchbearer short, and it had been decided by yet another official that the first Torchbearer of our group, who happened to be the 87 year old Olympian John Peake, would be required to walk the extra 300 metres which didn't seem to bother him too much as he strode away very sprightly carrying his lit torch and waving to the crowds and I'm sure enjoying every moment.

The Convoy Crescendo

Following our first Torchbearer was a great crescendo of traffic in a noisy convoy, which I'm sure would wake up the whole neighbourhood. I'd never seen so many police officers who were giving our first Torchbearer a metropolitan police escort. Also in the convoy were many police motorcars and even more police on motorbikes along with a bus, which we were told was full of the press and a television film crew. The whole scene was followed by ambulances and many other vehicles who seemed to be making as much noise as was humanly possible, which caused the whole atmosphere to be all smoke and fumes causing much coughing and pollution everywhere. Finally at the rear of the convoy was a shuttle bus which was to be used primarily as a pick up bus for all the Torchbearers who would have disembarked from our shuttle bus earlier, having completed their 300 metres and was then returning to the Key Theatre to collect their personal belongings.

My Grandstand View

Once our torch relay team had started it seemed only a matter of minutes before a further two Torchbearers, Nicholas Haste and Mike Russell, were departing from our shuttle bus at their exchange points on Oundle Road. Having successfully received the Olympic flame some Torchbearers would run but the majority would walk and it seemed only a matter of time before our shuttle bus was to reach the road junction between Oundle Road and London Road. While I was waiting for my turn to disembark from our bus I really did so appreciate the grandstand view of the great and glorious scene taking place before my very eyes. To see what was taking place, was most extraordinary, in view of the amount of people involved who were continually spilling over from the pavements onto the road in their quest to see the Olympic Torch. I really did consider myself extremely fortunate to be a witness of such a joyful occasion where huge and ecstatic crowds were giving a rapturous applause as the Olympic Torch was passing the enormous crowds in all its glory. The spectators really did go over the top in their enthusiasm of seeing a once in a lifetime moment − knowing full well they would never experience such a spectacle again. The joy on people's faces said it all and never in my life had I ever seen so many Union Jacks being waved most enthusiastically. I'm sure the many children present would say in their later years they had seen the Olympic Torch and would really treasure such a moment in their lives.

It was as though everyone in the vicinity of Oundle Road were standing outside their homes giving applause.

the vicar standing outside his parish church giving .... *applause*

excitable school children home from school giving .... *applause*

the publicans standing outside their pubs giving .... *applause*

even the ice-cream seller in his van giving .... *applause*

many shopkeepers standing outside their shops giving .... *applause*

the residents standing outside their hotel giving .... *applause*

customers standing outside the "Private" shop giving .... *applause*

factory workers outside the factory gate giving .... *applause*

and the local village Bobby out on his beat giving .... *applause*

young children in their mothers' arms were giving .... *applause*

There really was spontaneous applause everywhere, I'd never seen anything like it – how absolutely wonderful it was to see.

It Took My Breath Away

To see such huge crowds who had congregated at the Oundle Road and London Road junction literally took my breath away, which reminded me of the football fans of Peterborough United (The Posh) when at the final whistle the crowds would be coming out of the ground in droves from the London Road Football Ground. But I have to say that the Olympic Torch relay seemed to entice even more people as they gathered at this road junction in order to see the Olympic Torch being carried first by Charlotte Sissons and then Alice Evans, and the amount of spectators who had clapped and cheered from the Gordon Arms pub to that road junction must have run into many thousands. Once over the city river bridge I was amazed to see exceptional crowds in Bridge Street which is very much part of the city centre. People were standing shoulder to shoulder from one side of Bridge Street to the other side, which meant that this street was completely blocked because of the amount of spectators there packed in like sardines they were. On seeing this predicament I began to wonder how our shuttle bus was going to get through, but the police were very much aware of the situation and had managed to create a pathway a couple of yards wide amongst the crowds. It meant of course that our shuttle bus couldn't possibly go through the city centre which meant that three of our Torchbearers had to leave our shuttle bus with their torches, with one alight being the fourteen year old Sumayya Manji and Steve Berridge and one unknown Torchbearer and proceed on foot through this pathway of human bodies to find their exchange points in the city somewhere. I'm sure that one of the highlights for one of those fortunate Torchbearers would be walking through Cathedral Square with their Olympic Torch alight with the magnificent Peterborough Cathedral showing its prominence.

Where's The Convoy?

Because Bridge Street and Cathedral Square were experiencing a massive overspill of people it meant our shuttle bus had to be diverted away from the city centre by completely bypassing those overcrowded areas. So, our bus driver had to find another way in order to get me to St John's Street which is situated at the rear of the Cathedral. It was in St. John's Street that my exchange point was going to be, so on having disembarked from the shuttle bus with my torch I was simply raring to go, but I was growing impatient for the incoming Torchbearer to arrive. He being one of the three Torchbearers who we had dropped off earlier, but it was while I was waiting I was becoming increasingly more worried and somewhat frustrated that just maybe one of those Torchbearers had taken the wrong turning and was lost. I know it might sound ridiculous that such an incident could happen but previously, at all the exchange points that day, the transfer of the Olympic flame had always been completed at the appropriate time. But if the Torchbearer was lost – where on earth was the convoy? Lots of different thoughts kept coming in to my head such as 'with all those police in the convoy what was happening and where were they?' Another fear came to me which was that the authorities may have excluded me in their effort to make up for lost time by taking a different and quicker route, which they might well have done. But what I hadn't taken into account was the difficulties the three Torchbearers must have encountered in finding their exchange points amongst those enormous crowds, this being the obvious reason why this particular Olympic Torch relay was late. I should have realised this at the time instead of getting steamed up over something that was out of my control as I so desperately needed to get my legs moving so I could proceed with my walk of a lifetime.

Never In My Wildest Dreams

Finally (which seemed an eternity) the Torchbearer was in sight and sure enough being followed by the great convoy of traffic which could be heard in the distance long before I could actually see the convoy. By this time my pulse rate was racing with the adrenaline near to bursting as the Torchbearer closed in on me and then drew level. The Olympic flame was then transferred to my torch where I'm sure that every part of my body was tingling with uncontrolled excitement. So... here was my opportunity to carry the Olympic Torch – or was I dreaming? No I wasn't as this was for real and an opportunity of a lifetime. I felt so very privileged and honoured and never in my wildest dreams did I ever envisage or think it was remotely possible that I would one day carry the Olympic Torch. I thought pigs were more likely to fly than for me to be a Torchbearer for the forthcoming Olympic Games. As soon as my torch was lit and in my hands I felt a wave of optimism come over me and I really was very much alive for what I was required to do, and any nervousness I'd previously experienced before had disappeared completely as I intended to enjoy myself for this incredible opportunity I'd been given, which I knew would remain with me for the rest of my life, as I was indeed the most fortunate one to have been chosen ahead of thousands of other people who had been nominated like me. How lucky can one be? On saying my goodbyes to family and friends who had come to support me on such a phenomenal occasion, I was off! One such good friend was Sandra Jones who had nominated me for this event and for which I shall always be eternally grateful to her.

Emotionally Charged Spectators

So at last I really was off but this was not a marathon where at times I've struggled in years past to complete, no, this was a 300-metre walk of just a few hundred yards so I was hardly likely to get a sweat on. As I started walking along St John's Street it quickly became apparent that the big crowds I had previously seen that day had vanished and I couldn't understand why this should be – after all there were plenty of houses and flats in the vicinity. However, this situation was to alter most dramatically when my route ventured into Bishops

Road where I was literally confronted by hundreds of people – all of whom were clapping and cheering in a most vigorous way in joyous celebrations with once again, red, white and blue Union Jacks being very much evident as well. I heard my name being shouted but with all the noise going on I hadn't a clue as to who they were as the further I walked in Bishops Road the greater the crowds became, with spectators once again spilling over the pavements in their haste to see the Olympic Torch. To respond to these highly spirited spectators I was doing everything I'd been told to do, with the excitement multiplying every step of the way, which was to act like a stimulant to me as I began waving both arms in order to enjoy the happy environment – and fortunately my torch managed to stay alight! I do not exaggerate either when once again thousands of ecstatic faces from such emotionally charged spectators were creating a never to be forgotten atmosphere. I would have liked my walk to have been longer as I really did enjoy myself tremendously, but all good things in life do eventually come to an end where mine did, rather reluctantly. I carried my Olympic Torch for exactly twelve minutes before transferring my Olympic flame to the next Torchbearer. But what a wonderful twelve minutes it proved to be.

The next exchange point for the travels of the Olympic Torch took place near the entrance to The Lido swimming pool in the city when the Olympic flame from my torch was transferred to the last but one Torchbearer in our group who was Iain Crighton. The crowds by now had grown out of all proportion – so much so that when the Torchbearer had received the flame from my torch he seemed to disintegrate quite alarmingly having been swallowed up by the sheer magnitude of human bodies surrounding him as he made his way to the very last Torchbearer. So when my short walk had finished I had to find the shuttle bus in the convoy that had preceded me. Once on the shuttle bus my Olympic Torch was taken from me by an official who removed the cartridge which was still in the torch because without the cartridge the torch could never be lit up again. After settling on the bus and seeing all those familiar faces again bubbling over in their enthusiasm and reminiscing about their own particular experience, we all agreed this was a most fantastic and rewarding occurrence, which we would be unlikely to ever be involved with again and I was equally sure that being a Torchbearer all of us on that shuttle bus would be on a permanent high for months just thinking how fortunate we were to partake in such a project.

Lord Coe in Attendance

When the Torchbearer whom I'd passed the Olympic flame to had completed his walk, he then transferred the flame to the very last Torchbearer in our group who happened to be a budding young sports star Tash Applegate, aged 18 years old and well known locally in the city. This girl had undoubtedly the most prominent role of all the other Torchbearers as she would light the cauldron on the Embankment, which was situated behind the Key Theatre. The girl had a guard of honour supplied by the Scouts before running on to the stage where she was greeted by Lord Coe, a double Olympic Gold medallist himself and Chairman of the London 2012 Organising Committee. He probably had more to do with London hosting the Olympic Games than any other single individual.

According to the local press, official statistics revealed that 18,000 people had gathered that evening on the Embankment to see the young girl light the cauldron from her Olympic Torch, to much applause and on TV screens all over the county and other parts of the UK thousands more would be watching the celebrations which were about to begin. Lord Coe being the guest of honour at the ceremony held to mark the arrival of the Olympic Torch to Peterborough then addressed the crowds.

"It has been 46 days of extraordinary celebrations and today is a great example. Look at the turnout this evening as it captures the imaginations of the whole nation. Thank you for being here this evening, thank you for supporting great local people and thank you for supporting the Olympic Games."

The whole evening proved to be a spectacular success and I not only felt proud to be born in Peterborough, as the city had never witnessed anything like it before, but most of all Peterborough could be proud of itself.

As Good As It Gets

When I arrived back at the Key Theatre to collect my personal belongings, the Close Act theatre group were just beginning to entertain the crowds outside the theatre. Previously they had been entertaining the crowds at Cathedral Square and on the Embankment where giant puppets and witches on stilts were performing their acts. Youngsters I believe could have been startled by this spectacle with smoke and flares clouding the area, but those puppets actually created a truly magical atmosphere with children realising there was no need to be frightened actually enjoyed the proceedings. But it was when I emerged from inside the Key Theatre holding my Olympic Torch I was immediately surrounded by many excitable children who had made a beeline for me, if only to touch or hold the torch. With their parents looking on it was them who asked me if they could take photographs of their children holding the torch with me. Then in a short space of time I was encircled with literally dozens of kids whose parents were clicking merrily away with their cameras. This procedure went on for well over an hour and I must admit I'd found it difficult to refuse any of these youngsters as they might never get the opportunity to hold an Olympic Torch again.

Whilst all the hustle and bustle was going on I was being interviewed by a young girl from Radio Cambridgeshire but with all the excessive noise going on with much music blaring away, I'd found it difficult to concentrate. I did tell the interviewer that "I would be taking my Olympic Torch to bed with me that night," then the young girl gave me the most peculiar look imaginable as to whether to believe me or not. My wife and son then arrived and tried to get the excitable children in an orderly queue in order to stop all the shoving and pulling taking place. Even more children then arrived causing utter chaos. They had come from the Embankment where the entertainment had been put on especially for them, but as there were so many to keep under control my son decided it was time to collect his motor car. Fortunately he wasn't too long as I was becoming exhausted and was quite relieved to sit down as we drove home to Market Deeping – it really had been quite a day!

Later that evening at home I could not begin to comprehend the significance of what had actually happened on a most exceptional day. In fact I felt slightly overwhelmed by the consequence of the occasion and that I really had been a Torchbearer in my home town of Peterborough where I've lived in the area for most of my life. Having been involved in sport and continue to do so now, means that the award of having an Olympic Torch really is the icing on the cake so to speak as far as I'm concerned. Any trophies that I may have won playing sport over the years, in comparison to my Olympic Torch, pale into insignificance. Consequently what took place on 3rd July 2012 is now permanently instilled in my brain with continued memories of a quite amazing day that hopefully will never die. Maybe with the advancing years my memories might well begin to fade so I will look at my Olympic Torch to prove I really was a Torchbearer for the Olympic Games in 2012 which will always be a constant reminder that it really did happen. After my family, my Olympic Torch has become the most prized possession in the Holdich household. My lasting impression of such a memorable day really was that this is as good as it gets. I cannot possibly describe the day's events in any other way.

Market Deeping's Welcome

The very next day I was up early in the morning to greet the Olympic Torch relay on its arrival in Market Deeping. The torch had left Cathedral Square at 6.30am and was given an emotional farewell with literally hundreds of early risers, some still in their pyjamas, with school choirs singing and giving the torch a grand send off. Extra applause was given to one of the Torchbearers, a Royal Marine Commando Medic who lost a leg while serving in Afghanistan. Although I wasn't a Torchbearer anymore I was still sufficiently interested to see what sort of reception the Olympic Torch would receive in Market Deeping. It proved to be a wonderful welcome with hundreds lining the streets giving much applause by making their presence felt and I'm sure also the good citizens of Market Deeping really appreciated what they were seeing. I'm sure also it will be a long time before they will see its like again. What was of special interest to me was how my friend Shirley Waller would manage being blind and nearly in her eighties, but she did cope rather splendidly with help from friends walking with her, which really was an immense achievement and I know how she was appreciative of the crowds encouraging her on. What was slightly noticeable to me was that the convoy of traffic was considerably less than what I'd seen in Peterborough which unfortunately did not have quite the same effect, but that terrific atmosphere was still there and the only criticism I received was that the event was over far too quickly. Having passed through Market Deeping the Olympic Torch relay travelled north to Bourne and then Spalding and Kings Lynn. A couple of days later the Olympic Torch could be seen on the East coast.

A Joy to Behold

The excellent grandstand view I experienced whilst sitting on the shuttle bus and then later when I finished my 300-metre walk will live with me forever. Not just because I was enjoying the utmost privilege of just being there, but seeing such happiness on the streets was really unbelievable as literally thousands of people had broad smiles on their faces (no disgruntled people here) which said it all by what was taking place. The elation really was "a joy to behold." I've never in all my life seen such excitable people, which created such scenes of joyful celebrations. The residents of the city of Peterborough were clearly expressing their own feelings like those same feelings which were portrayed all over Great Britain for those fortunate enough to have seen the Olympic Torch. Just about every person I've spoken to concerning the two days whilst the Olympic Torch was in the city having nothing but praise for the City Council where the organisation of staging such a prestigious event was so brilliantly proficient – even down to the simplest detail. Special mention here should go to Annette Joyce, Head of the City Councils Operations Team who were heavily involved. This alone was a great achievement as the planning of such an event was inspirational.

On having praised Peterborough City Council I now find they have been criticised after it was learned that the cost of staging the Olympic Torch relay in the city was considerably more than the original quotation. Where spiralling costs are blamed for this situation may I remind those who have criticised the council that this was a once in a lifetime event for the city and is never likely to happen again, for goodness knows how many years, and even if the Olympic Games were to be hosted again in this country, it doesn't mean the Olympic Torch relay would necessarily come to Peterborough. As regards the criticism over the increased costs it could be that the council desperately wanted the event to be a success and in their enthusiasm may have unknowingly overspent. Let's not forget that for two whole days the eyes of the world had focused on Peterborough and like a good shop window the city was being thoroughly looked over, not just by the thousands who were fortunate to be watching the Olympic Torch relay but also television too. No wonder the council wanted to make a good impression of what Peterborough is capable of, which proved to be the ideal opportunity under such circumstances. Just ask any of the spectators who saw the Olympic Torch over these two incredible days in the city whether or not the overall cost of staging the Olympic Torch relay was really worth it. I'm sure they would reply that it was a spectacular success and well worth every single penny spent on it.

The 2012 Olympic Games

The success enjoyed by Great Britain in the London 2012 Olympic Games beginning on 27th July was magnificent, with record amounts of Gold Medals won by Team GB where it proved to be the most extraordinary games that the nation had ever been involved in. Where the agony and ecstasy of performing in the greatest sporting event in Great Britain since England won the football World Cup in 1966, where the latest success was so vividly portrayed on our TV screens and for those fortunate enough for just being there. By being

John Peake, No. 89

Nick Haste, No. 91

*Nick Haste - transferring the Olympic Flame from his torch
to Mike Russell, called "the kiss".*

Mike Russell, No. 92

Alice Evans, No. 94

Sumayya Manji, No. 95

Brian Holdich, The Author, No. 98

Iain Crighton, No. 99

*Tash Applegate transfers the flame from
her torch to set light to the cauldron.*

the host nation for the Games we had a certain advantage of performing on home soil and in front of home crowds, so when the Olympic Games opened, Team GB, over the allotted 17 days, accomplished far more than anyone dared hope for which was remarkable, and created enormous interest throughout the UK, where the achievements of British athletes each day produced fresh surprises as our Team GB made us proud of their performances which often produced spectacular results. It was even more pleasing because in recent Olympic Games Great Britain didn't always perform to their capabilities, although we had produced world famous athletes they didn't always reach the high hopes expected of them, where some would fail dismally.

For 17 days Team GB played out of their skins earning lavish praise as new heroes began to emerge which lifted the spirits in the cities, towns and villages throughout the UK. What was interesting was that people who wouldn't necessarily be interested in sport were often glued to their television sets and couldn't get enough of the Games. This was the overwhelming effect which seems to have happened everywhere. I'm sure that all Torchbearers played a very significant part in the fantastic success of the Games which set the tempo of what was to follow. The final count of medals won by Team GB in the Games was 65 with 29 Gold, 17 Silver and 19 Bronze with only U.S.A and China above us making Team GB a very respectable third in the medals table.

I actually believe that the unimaginable success of Great Britain's Olympic team was partly achieved by the astonishing reception the Torchbearers received throughout the UK. The sheer magnitude of the occasion happened to be colossal which brought crowds out in their thousands as I'm sure nobody could foresee that the Olympic Torch could possibly have such a desired effect. But the Olympic Torch did of course have a most important role to play as it was triumphantly paraded around the country which really was amazing, and nothing I've ever seen before or since has ever created such enormous interest because wherever the torch was the crowds would be giving stupendous applause as the Olympic Torch passed by them, as this insatiable interest turned out to be the ideal preparation for the success of such a forthcoming event, making all competitors, whatever sport they would be involved with, being well aware of what was expected of them, where hopefully they would be able to perform to the very best of their ability and where also they couldn't help but be caught up in the euphoria of such an awesome occasion.

The Union Jack

What was really wonderful and so inspirational for me was to be greeted by thousands of red, white and blue Union Jacks being waved most enthusiastically along my route as the Olympic Torch made its appearance, admittedly it was mostly the excitable children waving their Union Jacks but there were many adults also who were well and truly caught up in the euphoria of the occasion. As regards to the Union Jack, what an honour it must be for all British athletes standing on the podium having won an Olympic Gold Medal which has been hung around their neck with the Silver and Bronze medallists standing also on the podium either side of the British Gold medallist, then the Union Jack is slowly raised with their national anthem being played and in athletics every athlete whatever their nationality their big ambition is to win an Olympic Gold Medal and British athletes are no different. The achievement of a Britain winning a Gold Medal must be ranked as one of the greatest of accomplishments, the pride and joy there must be for a British man or woman standing on the podium is immense and so very emotional on such a monumental and deeply moving ceremony. So is it any wonder with the National Anthem being played displaying the Union Jack in all its glory that the British Gold Medallist is sometimes reduced to tears having achieved an ambition on the greatest possible stage. I'm not saying for one single moment that my experience of being a Torchbearer is hardly favourable to winning a Gold Medal which of course it's not, but seeing all those red, white and blue Union Jacks has given me a better understanding of what it means to have won an Olympic Gold Medal, because even on my short walk and seeing all those Union Jacks was very welcoming and if the Union Jack was replaced by something else it definitely wouldn't have the same effect as I'm sure those British athletes wouldn't like it either.

It was when I was in the army during my compulsory two years national service that I became conscious of the national flag of Great Britain, when I began to realize the significance of what the Union Jack stood for with its proud military history under the banner of this esteemed flag, just by looking at this flag gave me a reassurance that all was well in the world as the Union Jack was always a pleasurable sight to see, on the front cover of this book the colours of the Union Jack are vividly displayed and having been a torchbearer on that most illustrious of days when I was to witness thousands of national flags being waved filled with much elation. So in future whenever I set eyes on that magnificent looking Union Jack in all its glory I'll cast my mind back to that special day of 3rd July 2012, when the colours of Red, White and blue seemed to be everywhere showing its prominence, oh what a glorious sight to see the Union Jack fluttering in the breeze.

TORCHBEARERS' COMMENTS

Unfortunately, I was unable to trace two of the torchbearers who were part of the team I was in, for their comments of such a memorable day, having tried various different channels to find them but to no avail, which for me was so very disappointing as it hasn't really made this book complete. I had even written an article in the local Peterborough Telegraph, appealing for them to come forward but alas, nothing, so with one torch bearer, No. 90, who didn't turn up that day, along with the two who I haven't been able to make any contact with, No's 93 & 97, I have had to settle for the views of eight torchbearers, who seemed to be only too pleased to make a contribution to my book, where hopefully their own experiences of a never to be forgotten day will make interesting reading.

John Peake (Number 89)

John Peake of Stibbington was 87 years of age when the Olympic Torch Relay took place, being by far the oldest Torchbearer in the Peterborough area, and as a former Olympian himself it was just over 60 years from when he was picked for Great Britain in the London 1948 Olympic Games at hockey where he won a Silver Medal. He has had a most industrious career when on leaving school he attended University where he studied Mechanical Engineering and then trained for 4 years to become a Naval Architect, being a designer of ships. While at Naval College he was selected to play hockey for the Navy and Combined Services and then selected for the England Hockey Team.

In 1951 he moved to Peterborough to work for Baker Perkins and ended up 30 years later, first as the Managing Director and then Chairman of the Company and was awarded with a C.B.E for services to industry in 1984. To have reached High Office in industry and to play hockey for your Country really is some achievement. On such man is John Peake.

* * * *

John writes...

"I was delighted to be given the opportunity to be a Torchbearer by the British Olympic Association. This was because I was a member of the hockey team which won a silver medal at Wembley in the 1948 Olympic Games.

It was great news that I would be taking part in Peterborough where I had lived for 18 years before moving to Stibbington.

There was an initial gathering of all the Torchbearers in the Key Theatre. We were briefed very efficiently there and had a welcome opportunity to meet others taking part. A bus then took us all to the starting point on the Oundle Road into Peterborough just past the Nene Parkway Bridge.

I had been asked to do the first two sections since the person due to start off had fallen out. Having previously checked that I could trot rather than run most of the way I had to go a little more gingerly over the longer distance to be sure of arriving at the Shrewsbury Avenue traffic lights!

It was a great experience to see so many people there including youngsters. My thought was that perhaps this was because it was the starting point, but there were crowds cheering all the way along.

It was a great excuse for a gathering of our family from Coventry and Wimbledon. At the age of 87 I was the oldest

Torchbearers and one of my granddaughters shouted "Come on Granddad" when I started. The official next to her then said "Don't be rude"! When she explained that I really was her grandfather the runner concerned invited her to jog along with him which she enjoyed.

At my finishing point I re-boarded the bus which then dropped the next Torchbearer and was delighted to be carried right through to the end of the route. It was a great experience to see the huge numbers alongside waving the Torchbearers on their way.

We were able to retain our torches after its flame making equipment had been removed and I was very happy to be able to present mine to St Faith's, the prep school in Cambridge where I first became keen on playing games."

Nick Haste (Number 91)

Nick Haste is 26 years of age and was born in Peterborough and nominated to be a Torchbearer by his parents in view of the amount of money he has raised. He started early in fundraising when at the age of 17 he was Chairman of the group of students at Kings School, Peterborough, where a vast amount of money was raised including for one week alone £11,000 was raised for Charity. He has been employed in recent years by Wetherspoons in Peterborough where he was Duty Manager and has just recently been promoted and moved to Thetford in Norfolk as Manager. The Charity that Nick is mostly involved with is Clic Sargeant, which helps Children's illnesses like Leukaemia. He has raised thousands for this Charity by swimming in the River Thames and other hazardous pursuits. Well done young man, you deserved to be a Torchbearer.

Nick writes...

"July 3rd 2012 will be one of the most memorable days in my life. I was shocked when I learnt months earlier that I had been selected as a Torchbearer, after my family nominated me without my knowledge. The most memorable thing that sticks in my mind from the day is the crowds lining the pavements, in the rain, cheering and waving us on as if we were famous.

After joining other Torchbearers at the Key Theatre for a briefing we were taken by bus to our starting point to await the handover from the previous Torchbearer. As the bus was driving us to our drop off points you got a true sense of how many people had turned out to watch the torch and how well the torch relay was bringing the whole city and country together. Whilst we were on the bus we all introduced ourselves and explained how we had been nominated and what we had done to be selected. I can remember how incredible some of the other Torchbearer's stories were and more-over how humble and understated they were when telling those of us on the coach of some incredible achievements. I remember feeling very privileged to be amongst some truly remarkable people and just a little unworthy to be a part of the group.

I was dropped off in Oundle Road at the junction with Sugar Way. The whole time I was waiting the crowds were cheering and waving. Friends and family were all there and had come with a banner which said "Go Nick Go". People on both sides of Oundle Road all wanted to have a close look at the torch and take photographs with me and their children. Whilst I was waiting for the lit torch to come down the hill I was showing the torch to the children waiting in the rain and letting them take pictures, I can remember kneeling down to allow two small children to have their photos taken when a muddy dog tried to climb over my arms to get in the photo making a mess of the uniform. I can remember rolling up my sleeves to hide the mud and carrying on.

The excitement of the crowds seemed to reach a pitch when the torch procession arrived. There was a short delay for the handover whilst my torch was lit (which we had been told was a kiss) and then I was off. I jogged and waved to the crowds the whole way to the rendezvous point with the next Torchbearer, the junction of New Road and Oundle Road. I can remember being petrified as I saw the torch approaching that I would be the first Torchbearer to either trip over or drop the torch, fortunately that never happened. The crowd was cheering and waving the whole way, and it seemed my part was over all too quickly. The torch was much taller than I expected and somewhat heavier and as I tried to hold it as high as possible so everyone in the crowds could see it, from underneath it seemed to be even taller. The torch was on its way to the embankment where it was to finish for the night. It seemed like no time at all before I was being picked up by the follow-on bus. As I entered the bus everyone was clapping. I can't put into words how exciting and exhilarating the whole experience was.

While I was waiting to be picked up outside the Key Theatre, there was a succession of families with young, (and not so young), children all wanting to see and touch the torch. I had hundreds of photographs taken with the children of complete strangers, many of them with their parents too. It did round off a perfectly fantastic day, one that I will always remember. I was so privileged to be selected as a Torchbearer."

Mike Russell (Number 92)

Mike Russell was born in Brentford, London in 1935 and if anyone is more deserving than Mike to have been a Torchbearer, I've yet to meet them. Not that he has necessarily managed to raise a lot of money for Charities because he has not, but he has literally been an athlete all his life and utterly devoted to running marathons, and at the age of 78 he's already talking about his next marathon even though he's got a shoulder injury that he can't seem to shake off. Goodness knows how many marathons he's run as he doesn't seem to know himself. It was when he was in the RAF for 22 years he was probably at his best, where he ran many marathons in Germany. Although he has raised certain amounts of sponsorship money over the years it's his sheer love of running that he is so devoted to that I feel he is so well qualified to have been a Torchbearer. Apart from his family his other interest is enterprise which is all about embarking on new ventures, but if Mike can be seen running somewhere one will always see a happy man.

*　*　*　*

Mike writes...

"Having followed the progress of the Olympic Torch from the time it began its journey in England I found I was becoming more and more excited counting the months, days and eventually the hours as the excitement generated by the expected public began to reach me. With the honour and pride in which I felt by being involved in this historic event, having previously had the opportunity of carrying the Queens Message in three previous Commonwealth Games, where there were only a limited amount of members of the public watching, I never expected to see so many people along Oundle Road. My heartbeat increased when I saw the

first vehicles of the convoy come into view as the previous Torchbearer reached my exchange point and the Olympic flame was transferred to my torch, where at the start of my run I felt on cloud nine with family members and the public cheering me on with shouting and waving making me a hero even at my age.

This magnificent occasion has left me with everlasting memories as did the whole scenario from start to finish along with the achievement of all those who took part. I wish also to thank all who were involved in giving me such an opportunity to partake in the Olympic Games."

Alice Evans (Number 94)

Alice Evans was age 17 when she became a Torchbearer. She lives with her parents in Oakham in Rutland and is a student at Oakham School. She hopes to go to University and hopefully then to become a School Teacher. Her sports include badminton, swimming and occasionally cross country running. Alice was nominated to be a Torchbearer by a friend who knew how very active she was in raising certain amounts of money for Breast Cancer. I can only add that she is a most worthy candidate to have been a Torchbearer and most thoroughly deserved such an honour for one so young, and as she has written in her write-up she will cherish the memory of being a Torchbearer forever.

* * * *

Alice writes...

"Despite being in contact with the Olympic team well before the event, it still felt very surreal to be involved in the Torch Relay when the flame came through Peterborough on the 3rd July

41

2012. The whole day feels like a dream now, as I remember the excitement and nerves as my family left Oakham along with my friends Amy, Keera and Jack to support me on my leg of the journey. The buzz of Peterborough as it prepared for the torch to arrive was electric and as we wandered down to the Key Theatre to meet the rest of the Torchbearers' families and groups of people waited excitedly for the torch I remember seeing a poster explaining the route the torch would take which suddenly made the feeling very real.

On arrival at the Key Theatre I met the Torchbearers who would be running before and after me (which we needed to know for the exchange of the torches) and seeing my feelings reflected in everyone's faces put me at ease; everyone was very friendly. I asked one of the helpers how far we would run with the torch – he joked that it was a few miles and my heart sank as I felt that maybe I should've done some training! Luckily then he explained that it would be around 800m which isn't very far at all, but felt like a split second when I actually ran it.

I said my goodbyes to my family and friends and climbed aboard the Torchbearers bus, which was so exciting as the crowds cheered when we went past and I really felt at the heart of the Olympic spirit. At one point we became stuck in traffic, before we started the relay, and we all decided to talk about why we were nominated. The stories I heard of charity work and sporting heroes were inspiring and made us ready to run.

As each Torchbearer left the bus we gave them a huge cheer, as nerves built up again in the realisation it would be us soon! Finally my turn came and I spotted my mum in the crowd by the road because she had run to the spot where I would be (she later told me of how Sebastian Coe walked past her in the crowd which has never been confirmed but has become an Evans claim to fame). The sponsors went by with loud music which excited the crowd, and people asked for a few photos with me and the torch while we waited for the flame and police escorts to arrive.

My run started, and I can remember seeing a few friendly faces of family and friends I recognised. My legs felt like they were moving by themselves, I was so nervous but felt so happy and swept up in the Olympic spirit. I distinctly remember the police escorts telling me I was running too fast or too slow (it was a fine art apparently!) at one point I nearly set one of the officers on fire with the torch. My leg of the relay was over, and I felt exhilarated as I passed my flame over to the next person to complete their journey.

The whole day was amazing and the day made Peterborough feel at the heart of British pride in the Olympic Games. I am so honoured that I was chosen to be a Torchbearer and that day will be a memory that I will cherish forever."

Sumayya Manji (Number 95)

Sumayya Manji was 14 when she was nominated to be a Torchbearer and lives with her family in Peterborough. She was proposed due to the various volunteering work she does, especially in raising money through hosting different charitable events, and has been actively involved in the National Department of Education Youth Board where in 2011 she met two members of Parliament to discuss current issues facing youths today. Here is the example of yet another young person going to the most extraordinary of lengths, who is trying to help young people who are often disheartened that they have been unable to find employment, amongst other problems youngsters may have. Sumayya is well known in Peterborough for the work she does. I believe she was another worthy young person to be a Torchbearer and her account of her special day is brilliant. When I met her that day I was struck by her personality and intelligence as she seemed to be way beyond her years and I'm sure this young lady could make quite an impression in her life one day.

* * * *

Sumayya writes...

"England awaited 2012 with excitement. I remember watching the news eagerly, quickly realising the Olympic torch was not only running through Peterborough but staying overnight as well, a great honour for our city. It would be part of the link in history, a city that housed the flame relating back to the Greek times.

I never thought I would be one of the ambassadors making this part of history.

Every few seconds I would refresh my email, waiting for confirmation. Then one morning an e-mail: "I've been shortlisted!" I screamed down the phone to my family. Within seconds I had phone calls from radio stations about my nomination.

I first found out about the nominations when my mum saved a can of Coca Cola for me. She encouraged me to apply, always supportive of my volunteering and community work.

It is strange to think if it wasn't because of that drinks can, I would not have met so many inspiring people or taken part in THE local, national and global event.

It was a night's sleep until the 3rd of July, the day I had been waiting for. My Torchbearer's uniform hung on the back of my bedroom door.

A school day like no other, the evening ended in live television interviews, meeting people who inspire me and most importantly, a lot of memories.

I found myself immersed in ' a colourful Peterborough, especially the Embankment and the nerves kicked in. This was the day I would carry the Olympic flame through the historic Cathedral Square where Queen Catherine of Aragon, Henry VIII's first wife was buried. I met the other excited Torchbearers as I entered the meeting place and for the first time, I held the Olympic torch. It was a tremendous feeling.

The journey there was short, yet I made friends so quickly. Conversations flowed. The Peterborough Torchbearers talked to one another and learnt of each other's nomination stories.

One by one, a Torchbearer would leave the bus and start their relay with a golden flaming torch, screaming and cheers chasing after them.

Then it was my turn.

At 7.04pm on 3rd July, I carried the Olympic flame into Peterborough's most historical landmark, the Cathedral. Stepping off the bus, I was welcomed by flashes of photography and voices cheering me on. My torch was lit with torchbearer 94, Alice, and my journey began.

The crowds were waiting eagerly to catch a glimpse of the torch, waving. Waving at me! I felt like Royalty! I reached

Cathedral Square, where my friends and family were waiting as my relay was broadcast on the news channel. I could see my parents' proud faces, my two sisters cheering me on and my friends shouting out my name. I was so happy to be there. It felt like an experience like no other, one that I would treasure for future years to come.

After running into the Cathedral courtyard, the grand Cathedral welcoming me in, I met the next Torchbearer. Our torches were held together and the flame was transferred.

A beautiful day came to an end, after meeting Andy from Blue Peter who was presenting the Peterborough Olympic programme. It was such a memorable day, so many photos with family, friends and people eager to meet a Torchbearer.

Even after the flame was extinguished, I could still see the marks of the flame and I still refuse to clean my torch! Quickly, I was taken for another interview; I felt like I was in a dream.

The next day, someone said to me, "You're the Torchbearer!" Being an Olympic Torchbearer is not just for a day but holds a lifetime memory. So, yes, I am an Olympic Torchbearer!

And now a year on, the Olympic legacy still lives on and I cherish the moment that I carried the torch into the Cathedral Square, bringing history with me."

Stephen Berridge (Number 96)

Steve Berridge is a Site Manager attached to schools in Uppingham in the Rutland area where he has been very involved with young people, and also in the running of Youth Clubs all over Rutland for which it really does take up a lot of his time. I'm sure he enjoys his work as he's giving something back, particularly for youngsters who may well experience bad environment at home and hopefully to keep them off the streets. A keen footballer and cricketer who now manages the Under 15's Uppingham football team and next summer he will be manager of the Under 12's cricket team. Because of the amount of time he seems to spend with young people a family had nominated him to be a Torchbearer. Steve being modest was reluctant to accept as he prefers not to seek the limelight, and it was only through his wife Sue's persistence that he relented. Well played Steve.

* * * *

Steve writes...

"It was one of those things that you think would be nice, but will never happen is what I thought when official e-mails started arriving in my inbox. I thought it was polite to accept the nomination as much for the kind family that nominated me as I thought that a lot of people would love the opportunity and here I am with a once in a lifetime chance that I ought to take.

With the route announced my hometown of Uppingham appeared on the map and it really hit home that I could actually be chosen and how amazing it would be to carry the Olympic flame through the streets where I've lived all my life. As the relay drew closer I disappointed-ly discovered that I was in fact down to run in Peterborough. It didn't make sense (and still doesn't) why not Uppingham? By the time the courier delivered my official white and gold tracksuit I had watched many a days' relay on line, I had already discovered that I would run through the historic grounds of Peterborough Cathedral.

Tuesday 3ʳᵈ July finally arrived after a nervous nights' sleep and I went to work at my local school nervously anticipating what was to come, but being calmed and encouraged by kind words of both colleagues and students. After what seemed a long morning worrying about traffic and family arrangements I headed home to get ready after picking up my wife from school. After an event free journey we made our way to the Cathedral where we met up with my family, some had travelled from Hong Kong to be here and although the city centre wasn't particularly busy I could sense something was going to take place, but even I couldn't imagine how big it was going to be.

The time came when I had to make my way to the rendezvous point being the Key Theatre. I was immediately greeted by a friendly and efficient relay team who soon put me at ease and explained everything that was going to happen, where I was to meet the ten other Torchbearers, each with their own nomination story, secret nerves and ever growing realisation that they were soon to become part of history and what turned out to be one of the most successful Olympic Games held. After two hours of information and friendly chat the bus arrived to take us on a short journey out of the city centre to Orton as the crowds were beginning to build, children were waving and all of us were waving back, this was nothing though compared with our return journey to drop off the Torchbearers and the return by bus to the Key Theatre.

One by one the Torchbearers left the bus as at the same time the crowd grew bigger. It was here that I disembarked from the bus with Nos. 96 and 97. It was here that the relay lost the razzamatazz of the Torch Relay convoy and headed into the streets of the city centre. Wow, I now had together with No. 97 walk unescorted through the huge cheering crowds along Bridge Street with people hanging out of windows, standing on benches, it was amazing how the people of Peterborough had filled the streets to support the torch relay and to show warmth to total strangers.

Arriving at Cathedral Square which was heaving, where I managed to see the odd familiar face in the crowd and where I spoke to my wife and family. I was soon ushered into position as the crowd noise intensified and No. 95 arrived through the arch of Cathedral Square, there was the Olympic flame and it was my turn to carry it. Then off I went with the crowds cheering, people waving and smiling as I jogged along at a gentle pace, heading off for a rendezvous with No. 97. I immediately spotted my brother in the crowd with my son busily recording me on an iPad. As I headed away from the Cathedral the crowds were not as substantial, however by the time I reached city road it was heaving once more. Then there was No. 97 to take over the flame from my torch.

I'd done my moment to shine as the build-up organisers kept saying. It's hard to sum up how I felt as the run itself was a short moment in time that felt like forever. Then back on a bus to the Key Theatre, the enormity of the torch relay and what it meant to the people of Peterborough. As the crowds thronged towards the Embankment to celebrate the arrival of the Olympic Torch the bus crawled along at a snail's pace, I got off the bus with my torch where family and friends greeted me with many photos taken. This pattern was repeated over and over again and with my family made our way back to my car at the train station, I did, however stop off at the MacDonalds in Cathedral Square where my new and thankfully short-lived celebrity status lead me to be photographed with my torch quite a few times. Then it was back to Uppingham where my mum and sister had organised a reception at a pub in the town and still dressed to kill in my white tracksuit with the torch still firmly in my grasp what better way to round off an amazing day.

I went into this whole thing unsure whether or not to go through with it as I'm not somebody that enjoys the limelight. So therefore I must thank my wife Sue for making me realise that I would massively regret it if I didn't take the chance to take part. I was lucky enough to be chosen out of thousands of nominated people, to this day I still can't get over the outpouring of unconditional support, friendship and joy that greeted me when I ran through the streets of Peterborough carrying the Olympic Torch on July 3rd 2012. Thank you Peterborough and London 2012 you were amazing."

Iain Crighton (Number 99)

Ian Crighton from Peterborough was born in 1955 in Aberdeen, Scotland but doesn't really consider himself a Scot because he left Scotland at a very early age. At present he is Chairman of Peterborough Chamber of Commerce and has three multiple businesses, mostly in the motor trade and where he describes his occupation as a business owner. He really is a highly successful businessman and because of his work has few hobbies, but still likes a game of golf when he can afford the time. In years past he got a lot of pleasure when he became a champion rally driver. He is a trustee for Sports Aid East which produced Lewis Smith, a city athlete in gymnastics in the London 2012 Olympics and won a Gold and Silver Medal, of which Iain is quite proud. He is a married man with one daughter and two grandchildren. Considering his success as a businessman I feel he deserves to have been a Torchbearer and another most worthy participant. He was nominated by Peterborough City Council.

*   *   *   *

Iain writes...

"Signing a confidentiality agreement six months before the big event has a feeling of being something surreal. This was how it started, then nothing for months. It began to feel like carrying the Olympic Torch was a dream, and perhaps the organisers had forgotten I'd been nominated by Peterborough City Council.

But then it all started to happen – sizes for Torchbearer uniform, where to go, when to be there, did I want to keep the torch – silly question! Now watching the torch relay every day on the television, huge crowds of spectators, day in – day out! What if no-one in Peterborough comes out to watch.

Then the big day arrives and, much to my surprise, I feel nervous. Briefing at the Key Theatre and meeting the fellow Torchbearers, a complete cross section with young and old, all the courtesy of different organisations. The one thing in common was huge nervous smiles.

The Torchbearers coach arrives to take us all back down the route to the start of the Peterborough section, meeting the convoy and beginning our own personal journeys. The crowds are massive, at points along the route the Police have to move the crowd back to let us through. The spectators are having a party – music, barbecue, singing, dancing – must be the biggest feel-good event in the City's history.

One after another each Torchbearer has their moment to shine, dropped off by the coach, given their torch, ready to have it lit by their predecessor, and then 400 metres at the centre of everyone's attention.

The coach slowly empties and finally we're down to two, with me the penultimate Torch-bearer – even today it makes the hairs on the back of my neck rise!

51

Off the coach and the noise is overwhelming, and the torch isn't even lit yet. Each side of the road is packed with people cheering, clapping and asking to have their picture taken. The Torch outrider escorts remind me not to hand the torch over to anyone – they don't want to have to chase after someone to get it back!

The escorts move me back into the centre of the road ready for the Olympic Torch 'kiss', the passing of the flame to my torch.

Suddenly I'm on the move and I needn't have worried about how quick or how slow to run, it just feels right. Strange with all these people crowding the road, you still see family and friends!

All too soon I'm at the end of my stint and the Torch escorts tell me I'm two minutes early – I ran too quickly! - So I get the chance to show the torch to the crowd while we kill two minutes. Everything is timed to the second!

Now the 'kiss' and the flame is passed to the final runner of the day – Tash – and time for my flame to be extinguished!

Back onto another coach for the few hundred yards back to the finish, and everyone has a slightly stunned look on their faces. The torch is sadly decommissioned and returned to me in its own carry bag, to be jealously guarded and protected.

The plan is to meet my wife, daughter and grandchildren in the hospitality area, but – stepping off the coach a friend shouts, "Iain, can I see the torch?" And this is where I remain for the next hour and a half, with seemingly the whole world wanting their picture taken with the Olympic Torch. Salvation appeared to arrive in the shape of the Leader of the Council – Marco Cereste – who dragged me from the crowd saying that it was time for me to join my wife, who was still waiting patiently! Not quite that simple though – I was going nowhere until Marco had his picture taken with his family and the Torch!

Peterborough didn't let us down, thousands of people and the most unbelievable atmosphere, an absolute honour to be a part of something very special."

Tash Applegate (Number 100)

I finally tracked down Tash Applegate after many months of unsuccessfully trying to contact her, and as it was her who happened to be the last torchbearer in our team of eleven torchbearers I was anxious to see her in order to get her views on how she felt on lighting the cauldron from her Olympic torch in front of thousands of spectators on the embankment. What she told me was that it was absolutely thrilling when on climbing the stairs to the stage to light the cauldron in the presence of Lord Coe she did not want it to end as she was obviously enjoying herself. When I did make an appointment with her months after the torch relay I was undoubtedly amazed that she had managed to cram so much into her young life, particularly on the sports field either playing sports or coaching youngsters, she has become a sort of local celebrity and well known in the area primarily because of her love of helping underprivileged children play sports in order to better their lives, but its as a ladies footballer that she has become a prolific goal scorer in ladies football (move over Wayne Rooney) as she rattles in the goals at an alarming rate. Being a sports coach she hopes to go to America to coach youngsters at her own expense very soon. This young lady has unquestionably many deserving qualities for being a torchbearer and the C.V. of herself proves that, and boyfriends are out of contention right now. "I just haven't got the time," she told me.

Tash writes…

"It was my 18th birthday the day before I ran with the torch, so for me it was a double celebration.

I was nominated by my Mum's partner for all the work I do with children and adults trying to better their lives through sports. I have FA Level 1 & 2 Coaching certificates along with Emergency Aid, safeguarding Children and FA Youth Module Level 1 & 2. I am a qualified referee and have played football for over 10 years, scoring around 700 goals. I currently play football for Raunds Town Ladies. I coach and am assistant manager for my brother's football team, Wasps Blacks and also coach deaf football which is sponsored by Peterborough United. I gained a position with Vivacity shortly after running with the torch and now coach multi sports sessions in primary schools around Peterborough. I also work with stroke victims delivering rehabilitation in co-ordination and balance. I am a qualified Lifeguard and work at Jack Hunt Swimming Pool. I am studying Sports and Exercise Science at Peterborough Regional College which I am due to complete this year.

I was invited by Coca Cola to do a photo shoot in London in March 2012 with torch bearers from around the country. This was the first time I saw the uniform and loved it straight away. I also got the chance to hold a torch for the first time. We were joined by 'The Wanted' pop group and the photographs were on billboards, and the sides of buses, in London and other major cities in England and Wales.

My uniform arrived a few days before the event with the details of where I would be running. I learnt that I would be the last runner and responsible for lighting the cauldron. Although I felt nervous and full of emotion, I was 'over the moon' to realize that I had been given such a great privilege.

On the day of the event Mum dropped me off at The Key Theatre where I met the other torch bearers participating that day. As I boarded the bus I could see the torches and then the bus drove off to meet the flame at Nene Valley. Along the drive down Oundle Road people had already started to line the kerbs in anticipation of seeing the torch bearers. Once the first torch was lit we were on our way to enjoy the time of our lives. One by one the torch bearers departed the bus for their journey with huge crowds watching on. My heart was pumping faster and my thoughts turned to how excited and honoured I felt about this experience. It was my turn now and I stepped off the bus to be joined by Iain Crighton for the 'kissing' of the torches. There were thousands of people at the Embankment as the security team lead me to my starting position. I was scared of dropping the torch whilst running and held onto it really tightly. I could see lots of friends and family as I ran through the path that had been selected for me. I arrived at the foot of the stage and took a deep breath, or two, before climbing the steps to light the cauldron. By this time my emotions had gone to overload as after a countdown by the crowd, I lowered my torch towards the cauldron releasing the flame. I was overwhelmed with the amount of support, even on such a wet evening, that Peterborough had given me and it was the proudest moment of my life. Lord Coe then entered the stage and put a reassuring arm around me at which point I took another deep, satisfying, breath. Was I having a dream? If I was I never wanted to wake up, I felt I'd never experienced such feelings before as the world was such a beautiful place."

Thanks For The Memory

On reading the comments of the other Torchbearers it was noticeable that I wasn't the only one who suffered with nerves leading up to the event, where some freely admitted they also were full of nerves which was very consoling for me as I feared I might be the only one. Not that I suppose it mattered too much, but it really was an extra special day of the utmost proportion so one had to have nerves of steel not to be affected in some way. All the Torchbearers have written how much they had enjoyed the day and were completely bowled over by what has happened and wouldn't have missed the opportunity of seeing such an amazing spectacle of public display towards them for anything, which I'm sure will remain with them forever and at the same time realised how fortunate they were to be nominated in the first place, and like myself had come to the conclusion that such an abundance of friendly intimacy from the watching crowds, where it seemed everyone wanted to be our friend, with literally thousands of Peterborough residents boiling over in their enthusiasm giving loud applause involving much vocal encouragement from massive crowds spilling over, what an absolutely brilliant day it had been and I hope my reminiscing of such an event in Peterborough does justice to a quite exceptional day which hopefully gives a clear insight into the world of a Torchbearer.

Lord Coe wrote in the Olympic Torch Relay Handbook issued before the start of the Olympics "That all Torchbearers would play an important role in getting the UK ready to celebrate the Olympic Games". I'm sure that he would have been impressed with what he had seen where I think the Torchbearers' contribution was considerable, where the Land of Hope and Glory had produced a marvellous and memorable Olympic Games which really did exceed all expectations. I finish by saying it really was a great honour to be involved so "Thanks for the memory", the privilege was all mine. And I know I speak for all Torchbearers wherever they may be.